On This Day

*A Record of
What's Important*

Keeping Your Memories in On This Day

This book is not a calendar. It is not a journal. It is a permanent record of the important events in your life. In olden times, the front pages of a family bible were dedicated to births, marriages, and deaths. That practice has long fallen by the wayside, but the need for a personal and touching way to remember what happened on important dates remains. We have created On This Day to help you craft a loving place to keep track of things that are important to you. We hope On This Day will become a treasured part of your family's legacy.

You will notice each day of the year has a section, but the day of the week is not included because that changes each year. The constant is the DAY. For example, the first day of September is always September 1 but falls on different days of the week each year.

Here's how to use this beautiful book. For each important event in your life, go to the month/day it happened and write a note about it. For example, if your mother was born on June 13, go to that day's space and write her full name and birth year. Include whatever else is important and makes you happy. But, be sure to leave space in that day's section of the page for other things that might happen on that day in some future year - perhaps the birth of a great-grandchild, a baby's first steps, or a niece's graduation. You decide how much or how little information to include. There's space at the end of each month for things that didn't happen on an exact day. Just be sure to keep On This Day at hand for reference and to record what should be remembered.

I hope you will find On This Day - its purpose and the beauty of art and nature - inspiration for remembering.

My very best wishes,

Karen Engstrom Anderson
Lunde Designs

Nature Unveiling Herself Before Science by Louis-Ernest Barrieas.

January

1

2

3

4

5

Ice crystals on a window.

6

7

8

9

10

The Conciergerie, Paris, France.

January

11

12

13

14

15

Ceiling Painting by Marc Chagall. Palais Garnier, Paris, France.

January

16

17

18

19

20

Jellyfish.

21

_____

22

_____

23

_____

24

_____

25

_____

Lilac blossoms.

26

_____

27

_____

28

_____

29

_____

30

_____

The Nubians by Louis-Ernest Barrias.

January

31

The grave of Frederic Chopin. Pere Lachaise Cemetery. Paris, France.

February

1

2

3

4

5

Cherry blossoms.

6

_____

7

_____

8

_____

9

_____

10

_____

Mother and Child by Mary Cassatt.

February

11
_____

12
_____

13
_____

14
_____

15
_____

Mt. Rushmore, South Dakota.

16

_____

17

_____

18

_____

19

_____

20

_____

19th Century sculpture.

21

_____

22

_____

23

_____

24

_____

25

_____

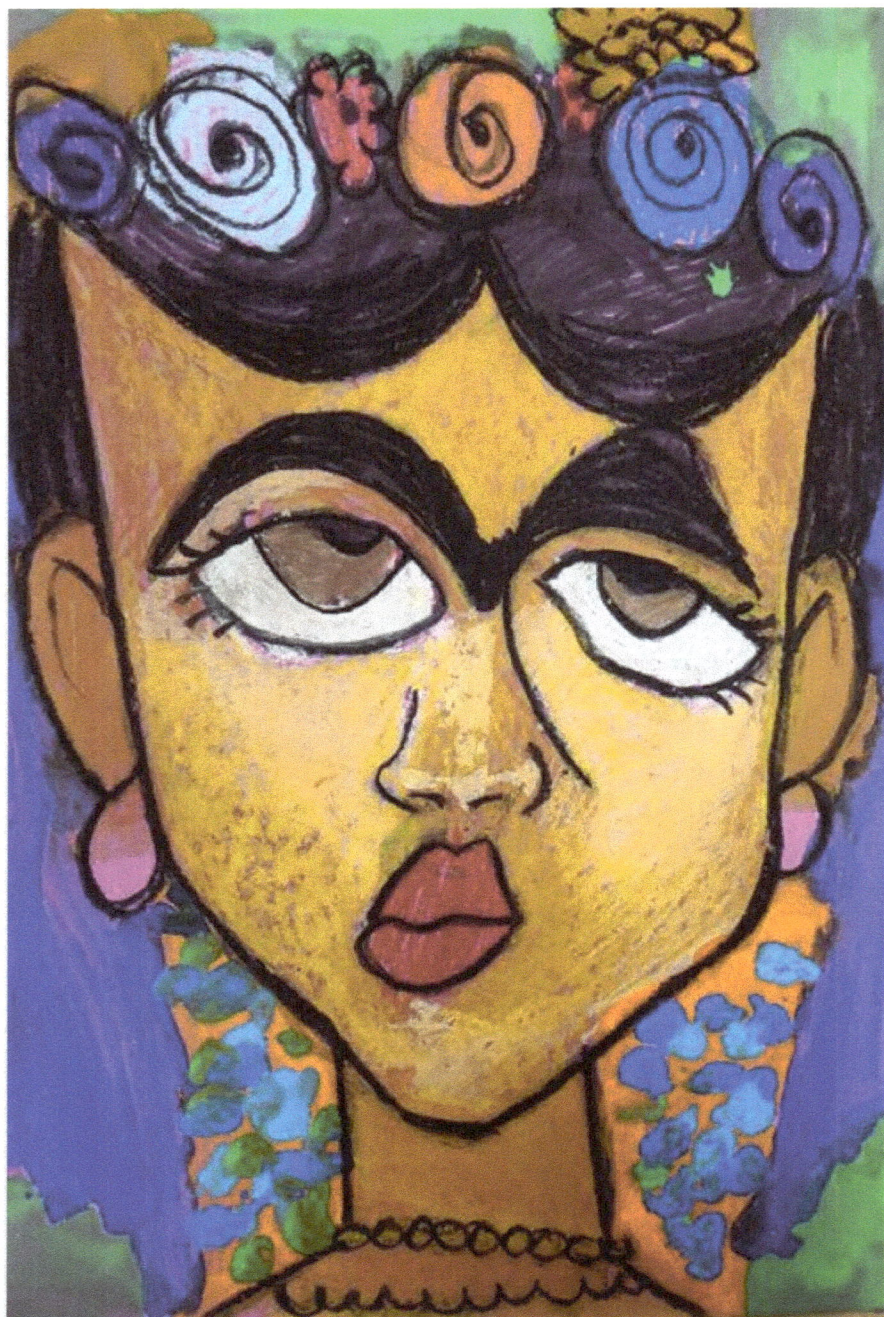

Frida Kahlo by Dupree Kingston Parks.

26

27

28

29

Aloe vera.

March

1
_____

2
_____

3
_____

4
_____

5
_____

Tawny Emperor Butterfly.

6

7

8

9

10

Haystacks by Claude Monet.

March

11
_____

12
_____

13
_____

14
_____

15
_____

Notre Dame Cathedral Door. Paris, France.

March

16

_____

17

_____

18

_____

19

_____

20

_____

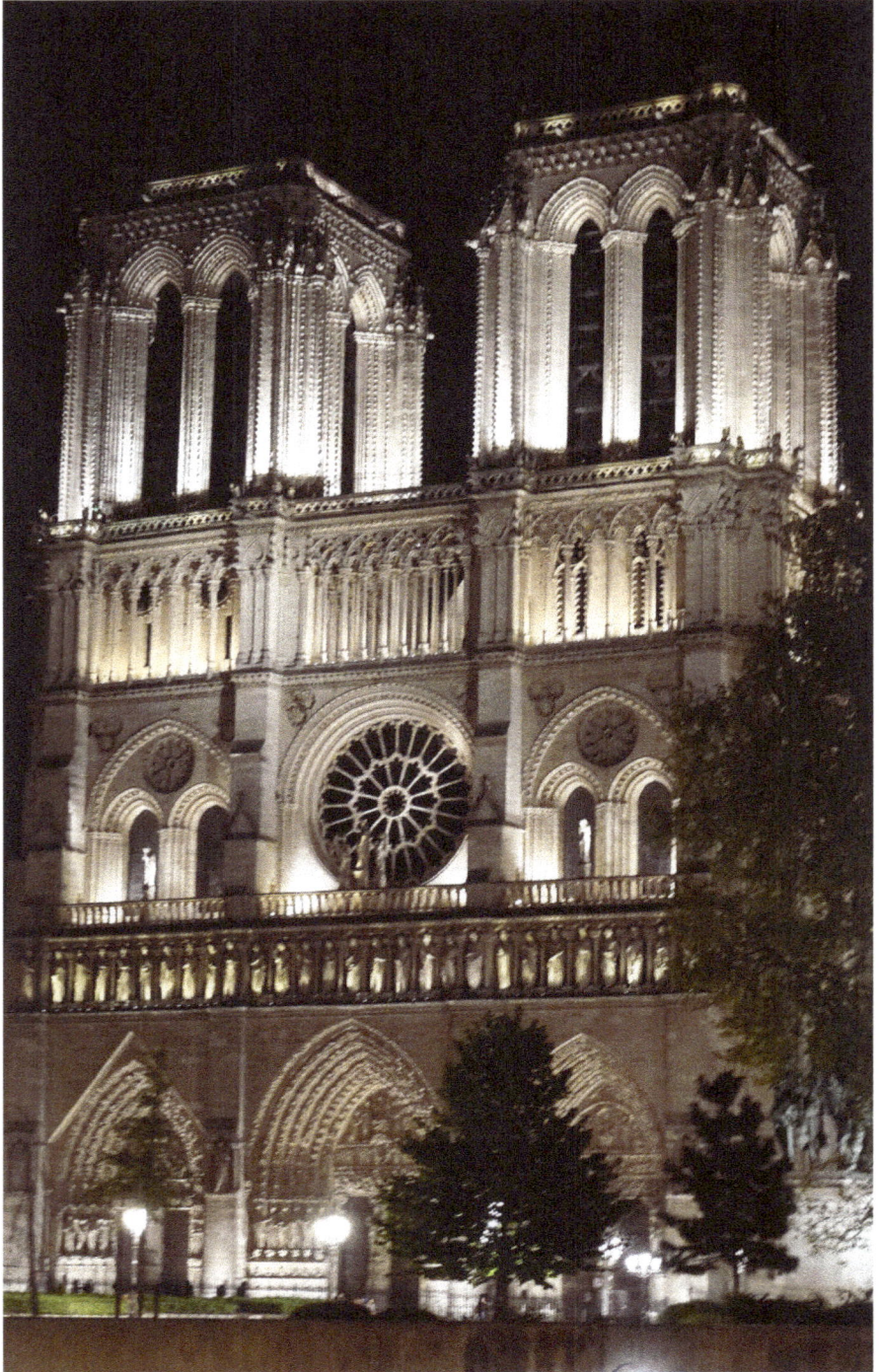

Notre Dame Cathedral. Paris, France.

March

21

_____

22

_____

23

_____

24

_____

25

_____

Frog by Leopold Chauveau.

26

_____

27

_____

28

_____

29

_____

30

_____

Sculpture. Musée d'Orsay.

March

31

Spiral staircase. Louvre. Paris, France.

April

1

2

3

4

5

Tombeau de Charles de Maigny by Pierre Bontemps.

6

7

8

9

10

Standing Horse by Edgar Degas.

April

11

12

13

14

15

Eiffel Tower.

April

16

17

18

19

20

Hoya Bella.

April

21

22

23

24

25

Tobago.

26

_____

27

_____

28

_____

29

_____

30

_____

The Times They are Achanging. Mural. Minneapolis, MN.

April

Dance at Bougival by Pierre-Auguste Renoir.

May

1

2

3

4

5

Leafy Sea Dragon.

6

_____

7

_____

8

_____

9

_____

10

_____

Marble slab.

May

11

12

13

14

15

Bedroom in Aries by Vincent van Gogh.

May

16
_____

17
_____

18
_____

19
_____

20
_____

Girls at the Piano by Pierre-Auguste Renoir.

May

21

_____

22

_____

23

_____

24

_____

25

_____

Pyracantha.

May

26

27

28

29

30

Harlequin and Pierrot by Andre Derain.

May

31

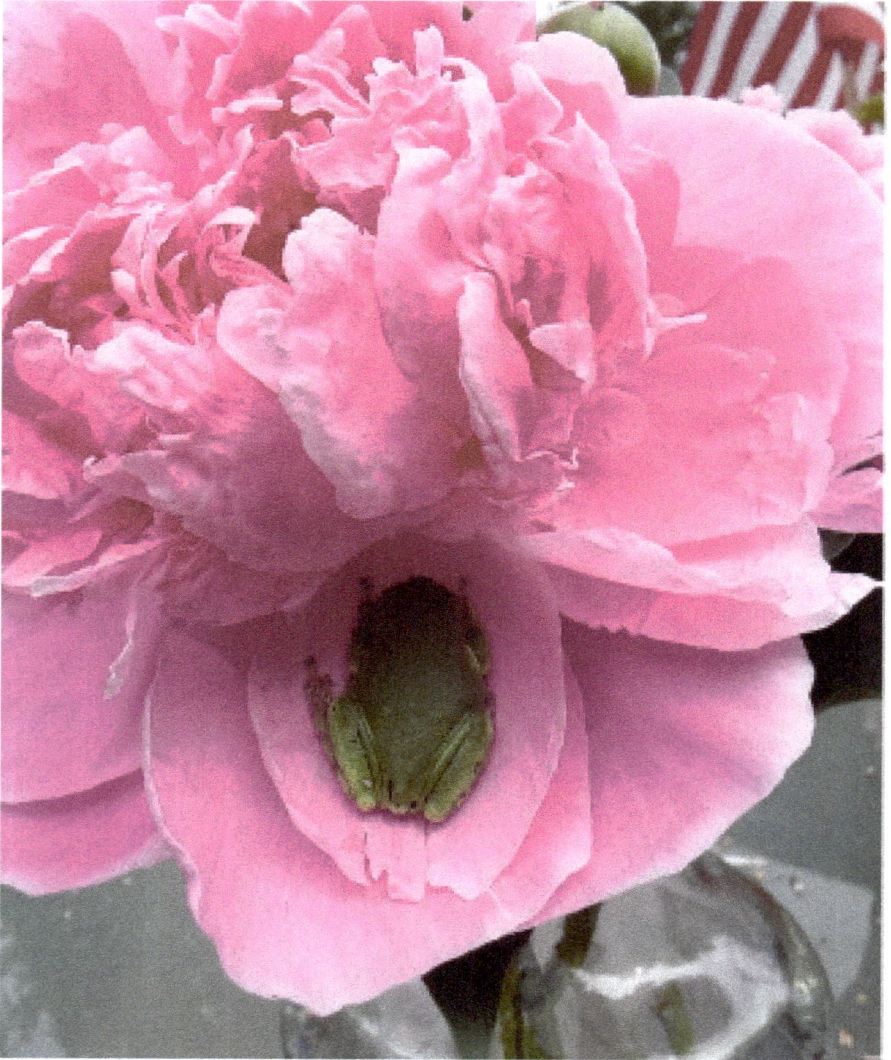

Begonia with Frog.

June

1

2

3

4

5

Statue on the Balcony Railing. Picasso Museum. Paris, France.

June

6

7

8

9

10

Aruba.

June

11

12

13

14

15

Statue. Musee Cognac-Jay. Paris, France.

June

16
_____

17
_____

18
_____

19
_____

20
_____

Woman with a Parasol by Claude Monet.

June

21

22

23

24

25

Architectural detail. Palais Garnier. Paris, France.

June

26
_____

27
_____

28
_____

29
_____

30
_____

The Kiss by Auguste Rodin.

June

Starry Night over the Rhone by Vincent van Gogh.

July

1
_____

2
_____

3
_____

4
_____

5
_____

Field of flowers before the storm.

July

6
_____

7
_____

8
_____

9
_____

10
_____

Christ's Entry into Brussels by James Ensor.

July

11

12

13

14

15

Devil's Tower, Wyoming.

July

16
_____

17
_____

18
_____

19
_____

20
_____

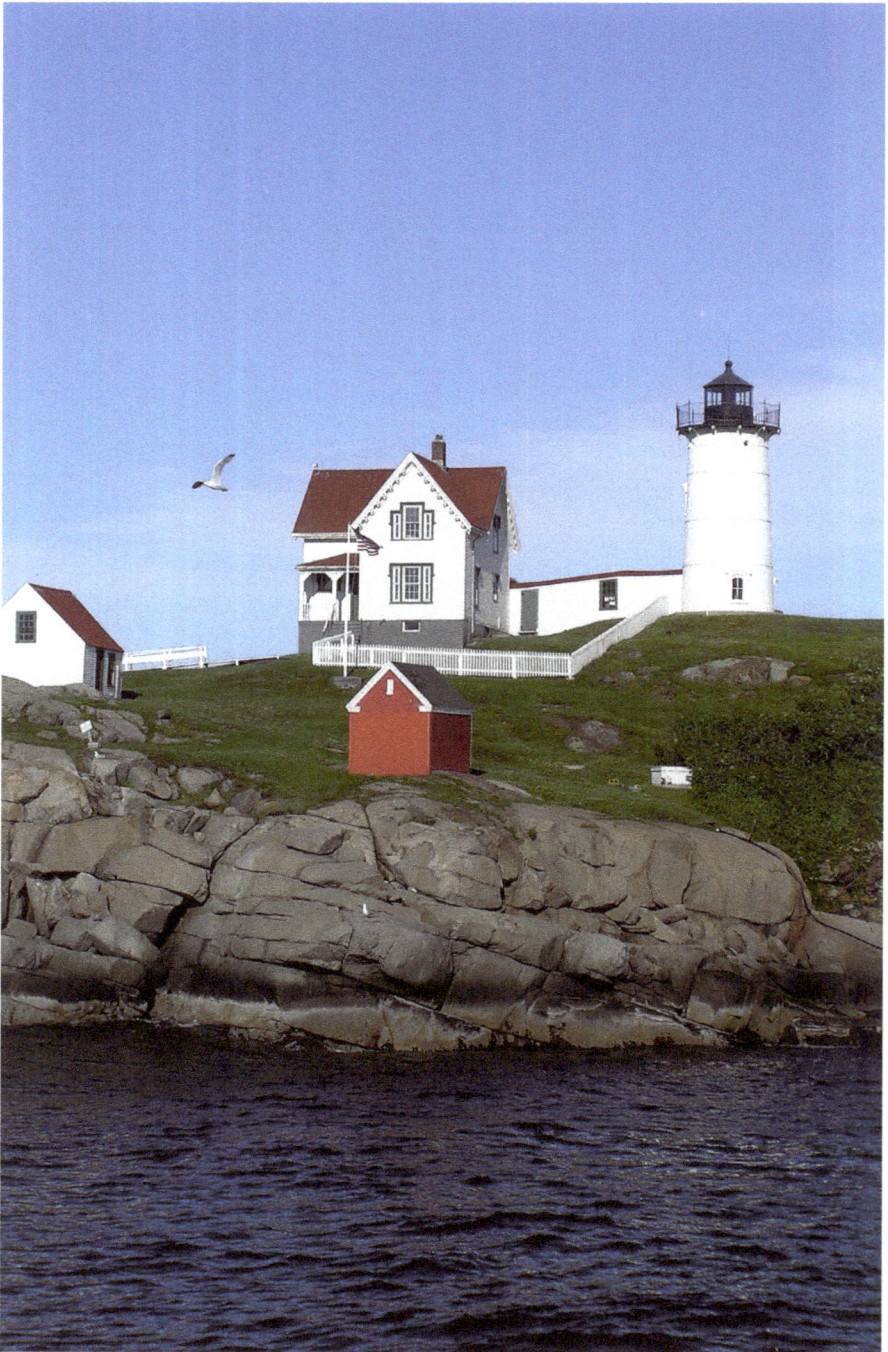

Nubble Lighthouse, York, Maine.

July

21
_____

22
_____

23
_____

24
_____

25
_____

Musée D'Orsay. Paris, France.

July

26
_____

27
_____

28
_____

29
_____

30
_____

Calibrachoa with honey bee.

July

31

The Garen of Doctor Gachet at Auvers by Vincent Van Gogh.

August

1

2

3

4

5

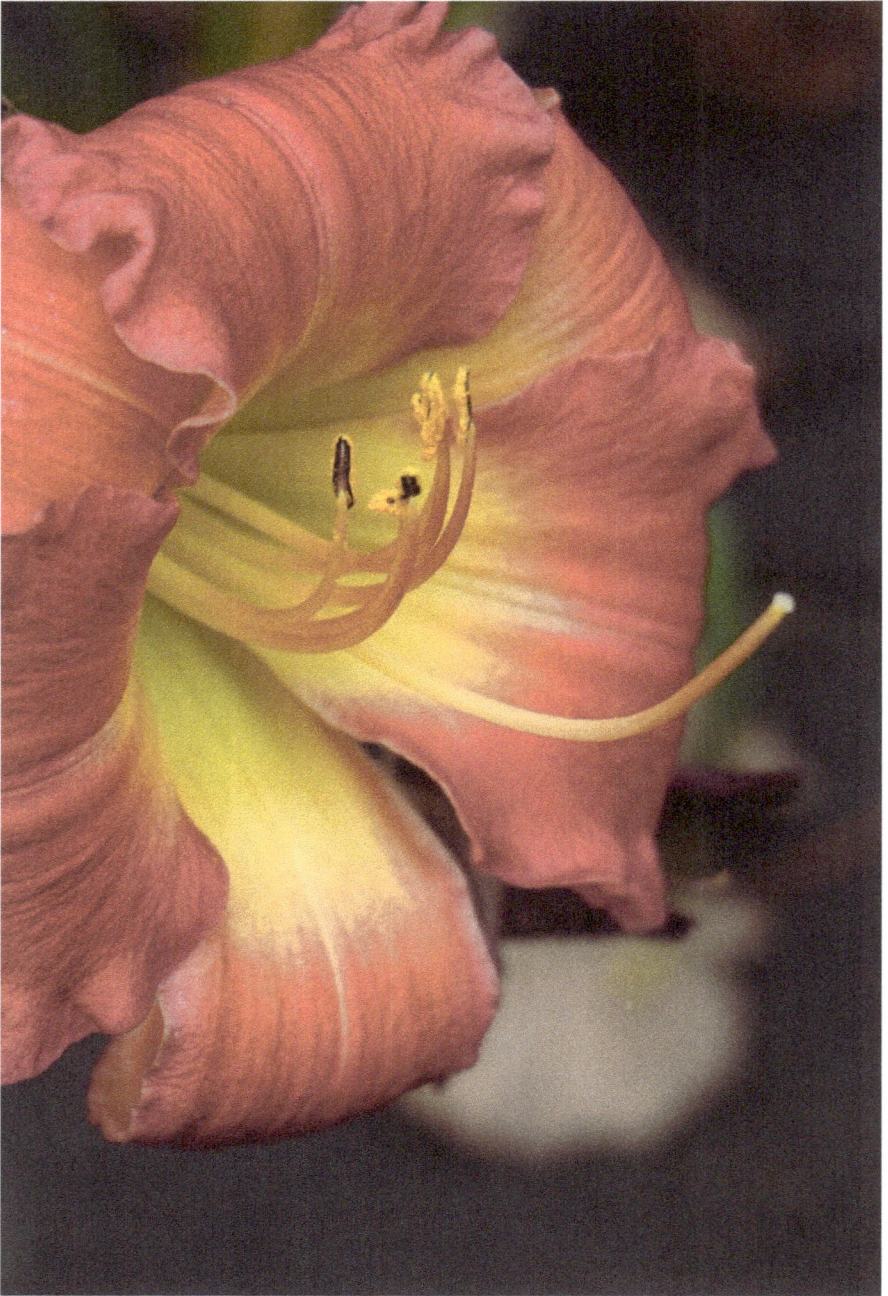

Day lily.

6

7

8

9

10

Tower Bridge. West Sacramento, California.

August

11

12

13

14

15

Wreck of the Hesperus.

August

16
_____

17
_____

18
_____

19
_____

20
_____

Sleeping Flamingo.

August

21

22

23

24

25

Phantom orchid.

26

27

28

29

30

Crane fly.

August

31

Ace of Cups by Salvador Dali.

1

2

3

4

5

Ibis.

6

7

8

9

10

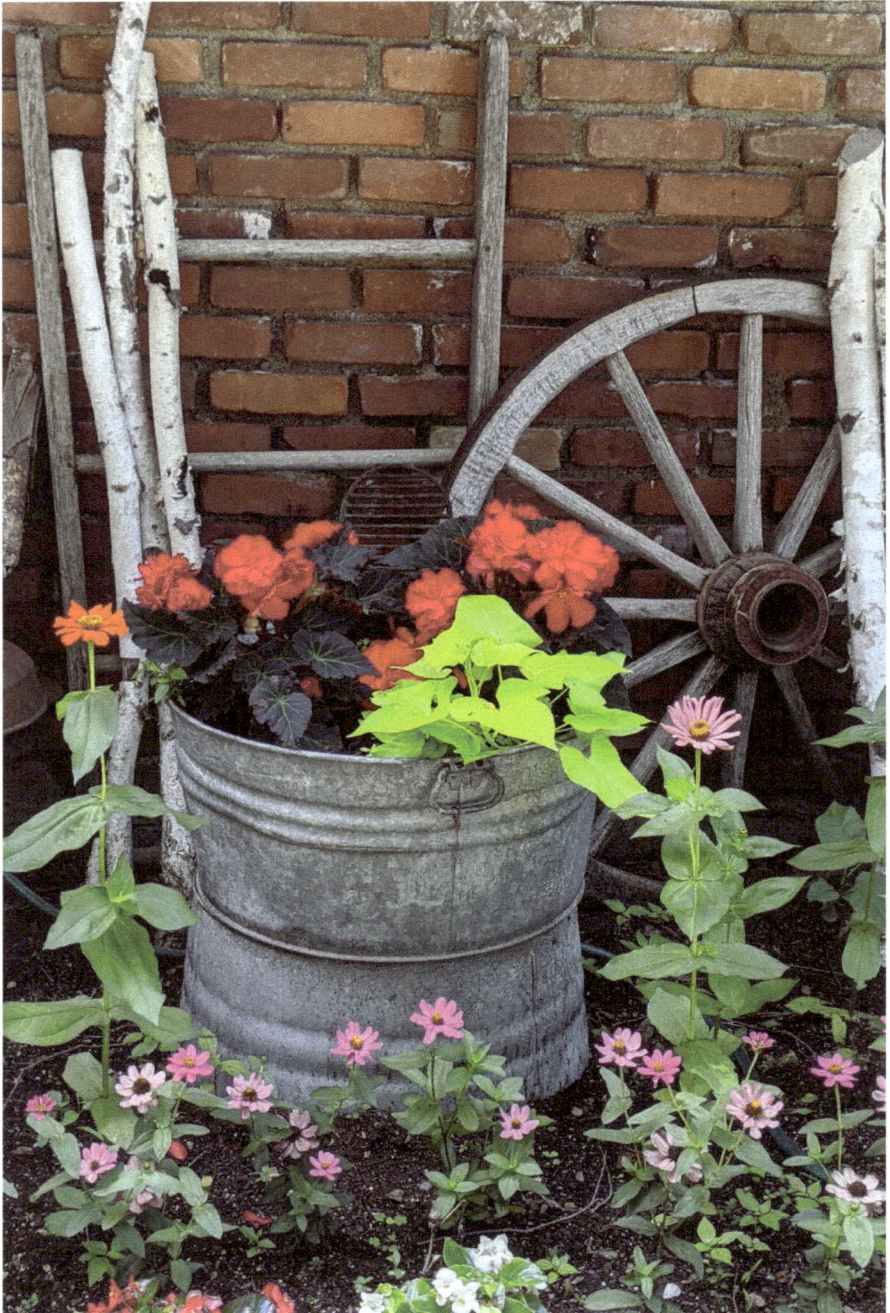

Rustic garden.

11

_____

12

_____

13

_____

14

_____

15

_____

Needlework.

16

17

18

19

20

Street scene by C. Jolley.

21

22

23

24

25

Badlands National Park. South Dakota.

26

_____

27

_____

28

_____

29

_____

30

_____

Redvein Abutilon.

September

The wood box.

October

1
_____

2
_____

3
_____

4
_____

5
_____

Paris Ferris Wheel.

October

6
_____

7
_____

8
_____

9
_____

10
_____

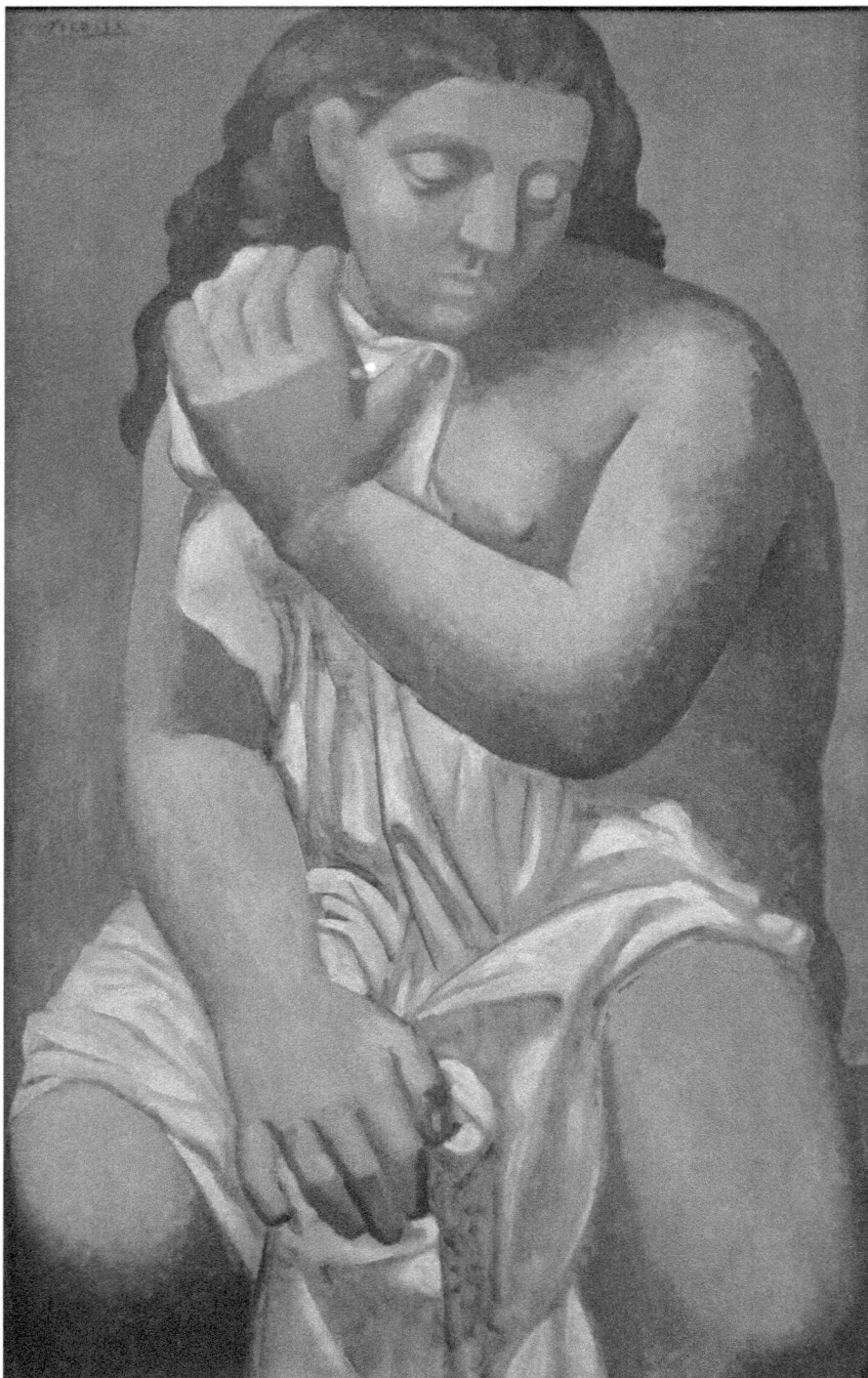

Large Nude in the Drapery by Pable Picasso.

11

_____

12

_____

13

_____

14

_____

15

_____

Waterlillies by Claude Monet.

16

17

18

19

20

Fallingwater. Mill Run, Pennsylvania. Frank Lloyd Wright.

21

_____

22

_____

23

_____

24

_____

25

_____

Lysefjord, Norway.

26

_____

27

_____

28

_____

29

_____

30

_____

Autumn.

October

31

_____

Wallace Monument architectural detail. Stirling, UK.

November

1

2

3

4

5

The Thinker by Auguste Rodin.

6

7

8

9

10

Portrait of Eugene Murer by Pierre-Auguste Renoir.

November

11

12

13

14

15

Maple leaves.

November

16

17

18

19

20

Amaryllis.

21

22

23

24

25

The Benedictions by Auguste Rodin.

November

26
_____

27
_____

28
_____

29
_____

30
_____

Florida.

November

_____

_____

_____

_____

_____

Lake of the Woods. Ontario, Canada.

December

1

2

3

4

5

Hoar frost.

6

_____

7

_____

8

_____

9

_____

10

_____

Banjo, the cat.

December

11

12

13

14

15

Cheval de Marly. Louvre. Paris, France.

December

16

17

18

19

20

Zouave by Bisa Butler. textile artwork.

21

_____

22

_____

23

_____

24

_____

25

_____

American beauty roses.

26

_____

27

_____

28

_____

29

_____

30

_____

Contemplation.

December

31